W9-BWD-878

Call Me When
You Find America

Doonesbury books by G.B. Trudeau

Still a Few Bugs in the System
The President Is a Lot Smarter Than You Think
But This War Had Such Promise
Call Me When You Find America
Guilty, Guilty, Guilty!
"What Do We Have for the Witnesses, Johnnie?"
Dare To Be Great, Ms. Caucus
Wouldn't a Gremlin Have Been More Sensible?
"Speaking of Inalienable Rights, Amy . . ."
You're Never Too Old for Nuts and Berries
An Especially Tricky People
As the Kid Goes for Broke
Stalking the Perfect Tan
"Any Grooming Hints for Your Fans, Rollie?"
But the Pension Fund Was Just Sitting There
We're Not Out of the Woods Yet
A Tad Overweight, but Violet Eyes to Die For
And That's My Final Offer!

In Large Format

The Doonesbury Chronicles
Doonesbury's Greatest Hits

a Doonesbury classic by

G B Trudeau.

Call Me When You Find America

An Owl Book **Holt, Rinehart and Winston / New York**

Copyright © 1971, 1972, 1973 by G.B. Trudeau

All rights reserved, including the right to reproduce
this book or portions thereof in any form.

Published by Holt, Rinehart and Winston,
383 Madison Avenue, New York, New York 10017.

Published simultaneously in Canada by Holt, Rinehart
and Winston of Canada, Limited.

Library of Congress Catalog Card Number: 73-3699

ISBN: 0-03-011031-9

Printed in the United States of America

The cartoons in this book have appeared in newspapers
in the United States and abroad under the auspices of
Universal Press Syndicate.

8   10   9   7

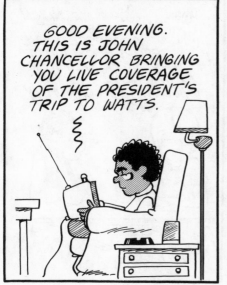

MS. CAUCUS, I STILL DON'T UNDERSTAND WHY YOU LEFT YOUR HUSBAND. DIDN'T YOU HAVE A NICE HOME AND LOVING CHILDREN?..

YES, BOOPSIE, BUT FOR ME, THE ROLE OF LITTLE HOMEMAKER WAS STIFLING. I SUDDENLY BECAME AWARE THAT I WAS DEFINING MYSELF STRICTLY IN TERMS OF OTHERS — MY HUSBAND AND KIDS.

IT BECAME IMPORTANT TO ME TO HAVE SOMETHING OF MY OWN, TO BE INVOLVED IN A PERSONAL PASSION..

OH, YES, I KNOW HOW IMPORTANT THAT IS..

I MYSELF AM ACTIVE IN THE AREA OF CHEERLEADING.

GBTrudeau

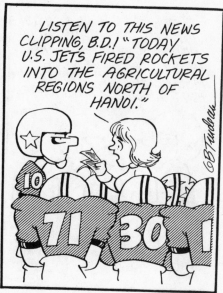

GOOD MORNING, DAD.

WAS THAT REMARK REALLY NECESSARY?

SORRY.